Handcuffed
To
JESUS

Handcuffed
To
JESUS

THE LIFE OF A
TRUE DISCIPLE

by

Guy Walton

Unless otherwise noted, all scripture quotations are from the *Holy
Bible, New King James Version*, copyright © 1979, 1980, 1982 by
Thomas Nelson, Inc. Nashville, Tennessee.

Published by:

McDougal & Associates
18896 Greenwell Springs Road
Greenwell Springs, LA 70739
www.ThePublishedWord.com

McDougal & Associates is dedicated to the spreading of
the Gospel of Jesus Christ to as many people as possible
in the shortest time possible.

ISBN 978-1-940461-20-5

Printed on demand in the US, the UK and Australia
For Worldwide Distribution

Contents

The Spirit of the Lord God is upon Me,

Because the Lord has anointed Me
To preach good tidings to the poor;
He has sent Me to heal the broken-hearted,
To proclaim liberty to the captives,
And the opening of the prison to those who are bound;
To proclaim the acceptable year of the Lord,
And the day of vengeance of our God;
To comfort all who mourn.

Isaiah 61:1-2

CHAPTER 1

My Testimony

I grew up in the streets of Lafayette, Louisiana, but I didn't come from a poor family. We weren't exactly rich, but my father was a very good provider, so we lived comfortably. My parents were prominent people with good morals.

Dad had been a Golden Glove champion boxer in his younger years, and he taught me how to fight. He always told me never to start a fight, but if I had to fight, I'd better finish it. By nature I was a very shy person, but by the time I was in the 4th grade I was in a fight almost every day at school. I never lost a fight, so I began to build a reputation, which grew throughout the north side of Lafayette and in a small town nearby called Carencro.

Aside from my fighting, I was an honor-roll student and very well mannered ... until the age 13, when I began to get involved with the wrong crowd. Then, as I began to enter into adolescence, I began to look for something to fill the emptiness I felt inside. Although my parents always gave me complete parental love, it wasn't enough to fulfill the need I experienced as I was becoming a man. What I didn't yet know was that the unconditional love I now desired and which God created all of us to have, could only be met through Him.

My Testimony

As thirteen-year-olds, a friend and I conned all of our schoolmates out of their lunch money and allowances, stole our dad's guns, and ran away from home. It was the middle of the winter, and we hid in an old abandoned house full of hay and started a fire to keep warm. The house caught on fire, and we both nearly burned to death. From there, we went on the run, and that was the beginning of my life of rebellion.

I began to experiment with drugs and sex, but they never fulfilled my desires, except for a short while. Then I had to do it again. At age 14 began street fighting and hanging out with the gangs in the high school I attended, looking for recognition and acceptance. At around 15 I began to smoke pot and trip on acid and made my first run to Houston, Texas to make a drug deal (which almost cost me my life).

Handcuffed to Jesus

By the time I was 16 I had already shot up my first shot of dope. As time went on, I built up quite a reputation, to the point that my photo was on the wall at the police station under a sign which said "LOCAL KNOWN HOOD." I thought that all of this would satisfy my manhood needs, but it only led me into more and deeper trouble.

My parents' nightmare of losing their son had begun. They were continually hurt and haunted by what I had become. They would lie awake at night wondering what I was doing and what was going to happen to me. They were scared to answer the phone anymore late at night, because they knew it was either the police, letting them know that I was in jail again, or maybe the one phone call they feared the most, that I was dead from a gunshot or drug overdose.

My Testimony

I spent my teenage years in the streets, and as I got older, I became a professional hustler and spread my name from Texas to Florida. My hunger to be somebody caused me to do whatever I had to do to be first. I was known for street fighting, pimping women, and hustling pool, but, most of all, for dealing drugs.

I was involved in witchcraft and sorcery and ended up making a statement to Satan that I would serve him if he gave me what I wanted. Although I didn't know what I was doing and really didn't mean that I would serve him, making that statement gave him the right to possess my soul. He began to use me to rob, kill, and destroy everyone and everything around me.

I now lost my mind and went crazy to the point of having a deadly temper, with no respect for another person's life, even the members of my own family. On two different occasions, I put a gun to my dad's head with the hammer cocked, ready to blow his head off, just because I didn't like what he was saying. I burned down my best friend's house with him, his wife, and his two children inside of it, out of vengeance for something he did. Thank God they all got out safely.

Everyone — from my friends, family, and enemies — were afraid to be around me, because I was unpredictable, and they didn't know what I might do next. Police officers were afraid to arrest me, because they knew that I always carried several guns and would use them and afterward go after their family, if I felt I had a grudge against them.

I wasn't your average drug dealer. I was a demon-possessed maniac, controlled by evil powers. Most of the times I had a large knife in my boot, a 38 revolver in my belt, a 38 derringer in my back pocket, and a 357 magnum in a shoulder holster, when I had a coat on. The main purpose of these was only to get me to my car, which always had a 41 magnum handgun with extra shells, an M-l rifle with two 30-round clips taped together and ready to fire, a short double-barrel 12 gauge shotgun, and a 7-shot 12 gauge riot gun loaded with double ought buckshot.

Everywhere I went I took along a Doberman Pincher that I had trained to guard my car and possessions and attack anyone I commanded it to. I had no feelings and no conscience. I had turned into a rebellious animal, ready to use my weapons at the drop of a hat, and I didn't care who I hurt in the process.

My partner and I were smuggling pounds of marijuana from Mexico to

Louisiana. He was in charge of getting them to Houston, and from there we would get them to Louisiana, where our headquarters was, and distribute them through other dealers around the state and in Mississippi. When he got killed, I switched from marijuana to hard narcotics and continued on my own, because dollar-for-dollar it was easier to transport large quantities of powder, because it wasn't as bulky. In the process, I dealt with the Mexican Mafia, a gang of bikers out of Houston called the Banditos, and several local drug manufacturers. I had access to seven laboratories which manufactured crystal meth (speed). That was also my drug of choice, which meant I could now do as much dope as I wanted.

The bigger my reputation got, the more power I seemed to have on the streets. I became obsessed with demonic power and deceived myself into believing that I could do anything I wanted to anybody, and no one could stop me. Satan made me think I was invincible.

I lost all morals and compassion, and all I thought of was feeding my demon-possessed soul with drugs and sex. I was trapped and couldn't get out. In the end, I became my own biggest customer and lost all credibility with other dealers, because I couldn't be trusted anymore.

Right before I began to reach the point of no return, I tried to make a big drug deal that I intended to retire on. I had enough dealers set up that I could break down a large shipment of dope and get the street value from it, and that would give me enough to start my life over and quit dealing.

I got greedy and didn't want to split any of it with anyone, so I didn't take any of my right-hand men with me, which meant I had no protection outside of my own ability to fight and shoot my way out of anything that might happen. The problem was that I had been awake for seven days, shooting up speed, and my mind wasn't at its best. My body was also worn out, and I was physically weak. I had no business trying to pull off a deal like that in the state of mind I was in, but all I could think about was more money and more dope.

Needless to say, the deal went bad. When I walked into the room where the deal was supposed to take place, five men threw down on me with guns. The leader hit me in the head with a pistol so hard that I flew from the foot of the bed to the headboard. I jumped up in a rage, but another man with a double-barreled 12 gauge shotgun was ready to unload both barrels into me. They put a gag in my mouth, tied my hands behind my back, and made me lie down face down on the floor.

I had enough sense at that moment to realize that I was outnumbered, and if I wanted to survive I had to use whatever wisdom my drug-infested mind could come up with, rather than try to use my own strength to fight my way out.

One of the men beat me some more, leaving deep gashes on my face and chipping some of my teeth. As I lay there on the floor, the carpet became red as my blood continued to pour out on it. They took my money, my diamonds, my car, and my guns and gave orders to one of the five to put a bullet in my head and throw me into the swamp where I could never be found.

On the way to the swamp, he took the gag out of my mouth, and I convinced

him that if he let me go, I would dis-
appear and wouldn't tell anyone anything, so he did.

After I was healed enough, I went
looking for those men with a vengeance.
I got word that the one who had let me
go was coming to a certain farm way
out in the country that night, so I went
there and waited to kill him.

When he got there, we began our
quarreling inside the house and decided to go outside and settle it. He went
out the kitchen door toward his car,
where his gun was. I threw the front
door open and ran into the yard, shooting toward him with my 41 magnum. I
couldn't see him, because it was dark,
but the fire that shot out of the pistol
made enough light that I could see
about where he was. At that point, I began shooting wildly, when I realized
my gun was getting empty. I jumped

behind a tree and reloaded, and when another man came running around the back of the house, I turned and fired at him.

This was what my life had become. I had only a few bullets left, and if I didn't slow down and use them wisely, I would quickly use up all of my chances and would face certain death. And that is how most of us are in our younger years. We take all of our shots in life very foolishly, and then, when we get older, we can only look back and wish we would have made better choices.

I tried to get off of drugs and sold my home and moved to Las Vegas, only to find myself flying into Houston to make one more deal. I was busted, with about $8,000 worth of drugs on me, and thrown in jail. And when I got out, it didn't take long before I picked up where I had left off.

Now I began to go downhill very fast and was no good for anything. I lost all of my connections and my ability to function intelligently. I then began to hire myself out to collect money from others, beat people, and would even kill them if it paid enough. I would rob drugstores for drugs and do anything else I had to. Toward the end of my crime spree, I was in a hotel when police learned that I was there. My girl looked out the window and saw police cars zooming in and surrounding the room. She screamed, "THE POLICE ARE HERE!"

I jumped up and saw the number of cars coming into the parking lot. Some of the officers were jumping out of their car and running toward the back of the building to make sure I didn't escape through a rear window. Immediately I flushed the cocaine I had left in the toilet and threw all my syringes out of the window. I hid my identification where they couldn't find it and threw my gun on the bed so they would see I was unarmed. They arrested me, but I convinced them I was my brother and bonded out under his name.

A week or so later, I was going to drop a load of cocaine off to a customer and was traveling down a country road between Lafayette and Opelousas, Louisiana, when I suddenly looked up through my windshield and said to God, "GOD, I DON'T KNOW YOU, BUT I'VE HEARD ABOUT YOU, AND I HEARD THAT YOU CAN GET ME OUT OF THIS. I'M ASKING YOU, GET ME OUT!" Two weeks later He answered me. I was arrested. I now know that it was God who caused me to steal a bright yellow racing helmet for a motorcycle that I couldn't even use because the color could be picked out a mile away. Besides that, I already had a helmet for my bike.

I was holding about seven grams of pure coke, along with guns and other contraband. My partner drove off in a solid black Satellite, which looked meaner than mean and faster than light, and I followed on my bike.

The car looked like something you would only see in an outlaw movie. When you looked at it, you could feel the power and the darkness that lurked about it. It would give you an indescribable thrill, which let you know you were entering into the fast lane, which would take you to the place of no return. Although it was going to be a breathtaking ride, you also knew that this car would bring you to your end. The strange thing was that even though I could feel all of this, I couldn't resist the challenge, and I got in the car.

As we drove down the road, my friend pulled into a convenience store and asked me for a shot of coke. I told him to wait a few minutes, because we were almost to our destination, and he could then have done as much as he wanted. But he insisted on doing some at that moment.

As I threw a gram into his lap, I noticed three police cars zooming down the road with sirens on, and I shouted that we had to get out of there. With that being said, I darted out on my motorcycle and got away, but the police surrounded him in the parking lot.

I was flying down the road full throttle when I saw what looked like an excellent place to hide behind some bushes in someone's yard. I darted off of the road and slid behind those bushes. I was waiting for the cops to come past me, but they had their hands full back at the store and didn't follow me.

So I was home free and clear, when I did something so incredibly stupid that it had to, once again, be God causing me to do it. I cranked off the bike and drove right past the store where the cops had my friend surrounded. One of them saw me on the road and pointed his finger and said, "Look, that's him!" They all jumped back into their cars and came after me.

In an effort to escape them, I went through a subdivision traveling at about 80 MPH, hoping to work my way to the interstate, so that I could climb it and jump it to get away from the police cars.

Three cars were behind me, with sirens blaring and lights flashing, when I came to a T where I had to turn either left or right. I tried to turn right toward the interstate by locking my brakes up and skidding with the front end facing the right. I down-shifted the bike into a low gear, so that I could let the clutch go with full throttle, which would cause the bike to spin the back wheel, to build up enough momentum to dart out in that direction.

If I judged the distance right, I would be able to drop my speed down from 80 MPH to a slow enough speed, and with the tires spinning, I would make the turn. If I misjudged, I would wipe out. As I was about to let the clutch go, a police car came out of nowhere and blocked that lane, so I couldn't turn.

With just a couple of seconds left before I crashed into the truck stopped at the intersection, I pulled upward on the bike with all of my strength, to bring it upright on two wheels again. I then threw it hard to the left in hopes that I had enough time to maneuver it, to do the same thing, except in the opposite direction.

Just then another police car came out of nowhere from the other direction and blocked that way. The bike was now skidding on its left side, which left me with no alternatives but to hang on to the handlebars, stand on the side of the bike that was facing up, and ride it to the end of the road.

At the end of the road was the T, which meant that I ended up in the ditch. When the bike hit the ditch, I jumped off and ran about ten feet, reaching in my belt for my pistol, and I heard one of the officers shout, "He's reaching for something!"

After that I only heard shotguns, rifles, and pistols cocking the hammers back and putting a bullet in their gun's chamber, and I knew in that moment that I was a goner if I made one wrong move. So, I immediately threw my gun to the ground and hit the ground face down under the command of the officers. They quickly surrounded me, handcuffed me, and hauled me off to the station.

Even though I did not yet know it, God was causing all of this to happen because I had prayed and asked Him to save me from that terrible lifestyle. His plan included me going to jail, where a lady would come several times a week to minister the Gospel, and she gave me a Bible.

God used this woman to reunite me with my family and to find my way to Jesus. I went to a halfway house for six months and then moved to Houma, Louisiana, and stayed at my grandmother's home for a while, as I tried to get my life together.

Handcuffed to Jesus

As I was driving past the Living Word Church in Houma one day, God grabbed my steering wheel and turned the car into their parking lot. I tried to stop the steering wheel from turning, but He is much stronger than I am, so He won.

When the car pulled up to the church, I knew I was supposed to get out and go inside, so I did. I met the pastor, and he led me to true salvation and taught me everything in the Bible and how to hear God's voice. It was a long hard road, but it was worth it.

In the beginning, God spoke to me and told me that if I stayed with Him, He would heal my body and soul and give me back everything that had been taken from me. From 1983 until now I have been ministering the Gospel in every place Satan once used me to destroy so many lives. When I met my wife,

My Testimony

Maria, we got married immediately on February 23, 1993, and have been ministering together ever since.

God gave us a prison ministry, through which we have gone into every state prison in south Louisiana. He sent us to Mexico, where I had been involved in smuggling drugs, and used us to build a children's home. He used us to start several churches and evangelize the streets of New Orleans and Lafayette, where I had sold drugs and pimped women. Today we are building another orphanage in Kenya. (For more information, visit our web site at www. TrueLifeOfLa.com).

We have seen God heal every sort of sickness on the streets, open blind eyes, raise people out of their wheelchairs, heal deaf ears, and so many other miracles I couldn't name them all. Now we are fulfilling His last assignment, which is to build churches the same way they were built in the book of Acts.

We are training fivefold ministers to serve God in house churches, and this brings us to this book entitled *Handcuffed to Jesus*. We wrote it to explain the true disciple scriptures and how to live in the full power of the Holy Spirit.

CHAPTER 2

The Warning of God

Close to two thousand years ago God came upon the earth in the form of a Man to tell us how much He loves us and to give His life for us (Philippians 2:5-8) that we may have eternal life (John 3:16) and power over all evil, with protection from any harm (Luke 10:19).

Throughout His life this Man never did one thing to bring harm to anyone. He only did what was necessary to help those who were lost to find their way. It doesn't matter to Him what anyone has ever done, He loves all unconditionally, even to the point that He Himself gave His life so that all could be forgiven. His name is Jesus Christ.

From the day that He was on the earth, people have hated Him because He told us the truth about our sinful ways. Now that we know that we have to quit doing what is sinful, we have no excuse to continue in sin. Instead of being grateful to Him for showing us the way, many hate Him without a cause to do so (John 15:22-25) simply because He exposed the truth to them, which showed them their way of living was wrong.

In the beginning, people did everything in their power to kill and destroy Him, and today it is no different. Even some who call themselves Christians don't seem to take what it means to represent Him seriously. Jesus didn't come to do away with God's law, but to fulfill it (Matthew 5:17), which means that in the New Testament the price has gone up to be a Christian.

When I was of the world, I did a lot of things that were downright sinful. I also did a lot of things that I believed were permissible, as far as being right or wrong goes, such as telling white lies, gossiping, cheating on my income tax, watching dirty movies or magazines when no one was looking, breaking the simple laws, like speeding, etc., which I now know is sin in the eyes of God.

I did everything I could and worked very hard to make enough money to buy the things I wanted in life, things that, sooner or later, would be lost back to the same world they came from. I was willing to spend my life trying to get something I thought was worthy, because it was something I wanted, even though I didn't really need it.

The same thing is happening in the lives of a lot of people today, including Christians. They are willing to lay their lives down and work hard all of their lives so they can have a good retirement on this earth and buy worldly goods, instead of giving their lives to Jesus and living to further His Kingdom.

This is the same as in the days of Noah. When he lived, the whole earth was filled with sinful people, rebelling against the ways of God. God was grieved in His heart from man's wickedness and decided to destroy all who would not follow Him. Only Noah and his family found grace in the eyes of the Lord (Genesis 6:7-8) because he obeyed all that God commanded him to do (Genesis 6:22-7:1).

The Warning of God

God told Noah that he was planning to destroy the world and told him to build an ark for him and his family to escape from the flood (Genesis 6:14). Noah heard God's warning and obeyed Him.

Just as it is happening today, God warned all of what was coming, but no one listened. God didn't pull the plug on everyone sudden like. He allowed Noah to work on the ark and preach the Word for one hundred and twenty years. Through that whole time, everyone carried on like nothing bad would really happen, and all but eight souls were lost (1 Peter 3:20).

God has given us nearly two thousand years to line up with His commandments, allowing us to have a church on every corner, put people preaching on the street corners. We have twenty-four-hour Christian television and radio, and most of us still don't take His Word seriously.

He didn't spare the angels who sinned or anyone else from the ancient world except Noah and his family (2 Peter 2:4-5). So what makes people think they will escape judgment if they aren't righteous today?

Many who do make it to Heaven will be bankrupt, with no treasures awaiting them. They will have to go through eternity with nothing because they have had no foresight and chose to live for this world instead of the world to come. They will have relied on man's knowledge and reasoning of what success is instead of what God says (Colossians 2:8), and therefore they will be cheated out of the real treasure.

CHAPTER 3

Where Is Your Heart?

Do not lay up for yourselves treasures on earth, where moth and rust destroy and where thieves break in and steal; but lay up for yourselves treasures in heaven, where neither moth nor rust destroys and where thieves do not break in and steal. For where your treasure is, there your heart will be also.

Matthew 6:19-21

God isn't saying that it is wrong to seek a good career and make a lot of money.

He isn't saying that we shouldn't have a comfortable house and nice things for our family. He wants us to have the best of everything.

However, there is a difference between buying a house that will fully meet all of your needs comfortably and going overboard and buying a mansion. There's a difference between wanting a nice car and buying a Rolls Royce instead of some other nice car that will do the job for much less.

If we are wise and Jesus is truly our Lord, we will not go to the extremes of this world and will buy only what we need to live comfortably and put the difference of the cost into furthering God's Kingdom. Buying things just to have them is very selfish and totally out of God's will.

If we want to be perfect in God's eyes, we must take what we have and help the poor and follow Jesus. By doing this, we will have treasures in Heaven (Matthew 19:21).

Jesus even told the rich young ruler in Luke 18:18-25 that he must sell all that he had and distribute it to the poor to have treasure in Heaven and follow Him in order to have eternal life. Unfortunately the man trusted in his money more than in God, and so he missed the mark.

There is a definite distinction between the ones who just want the benefits of being a Christian and those who truly have made Jesus Lord of their lives. The rich young ruler wanted the benefits of eternal life, but wasn't willing to give up his worldly treasures. In Acts 2:37-47, we see an example of people who were truly transformed into the image of Christ.

In the time of the early Church, the believers truly repented and were saved.

As a result of them allowing the Holy Spirit to fully change them, they continued steadfastly in the instructions they received of the new life (v. 42) and many miracles were done (v. 43).

They became as Jesus and loved one another to the point of putting others ahead of themselves. They sold their possessions and goods and divided the proceeds to each other as was needed (v. 45). Because of their obedience of love and giving, the Lord added souls to the Church daily.

God wants us to love one another as we love ourselves (Mark 12:31). He did not mean for us to be so selfish that we would sit in a nice comfortable home with food in the freezer and money in the bank while our brothers and sisters in Christ are starving all over the land.

This only shows where the church's heart is. John wrote to the churches,

Where Is Your Heart?

"But whoever has this world's goods, and sees his brother in need, and shuts up his heart from him, how does the love of God abide in him?" (1 John 3:17).

If we are truly Christians (meaning Christ-like, followers of Jesus), we should have a hard time saving all of our money in the bank, when it could be used to reach the millions of sinners who are going to go to Hell if they die without Christ. How can people be so selfish and still confess Jesus as their Lord?

God commands us to love our neighbor as ourselves (Mark 12:31), and yet there are so many who are willing to save their money for their own pleasures, when so many of our brothers and sisters are starving and in need.

God is our provider, and He is our King. If He is truly our Lord, then we should use everything we have over our present needs to further the Gospel, as

He desires us to do, and then trust Him to meet the next need. He doesn't want us to build up large bank accounts and get dependent upon our money to get us through.

Because the widow in 1 Kings 17:8-16 obeyed what Elijah told her to do and made him a small cake from her last bit of flour and oil before she cooked a last meal for herself and her son (v. 13), God blessed them with food that never ran out (v. 16), even when there was a severe drought, which brought a loss of food throughout the land.

Most people believe that they should save so they can have a nice inheritance for their children. This is true, but most people have their eyes on the wrong thing as far as what is the best inheritance for their children.

If you owned the whole world, you would be able to give your children the best of everything and give them anything. Unfortunately neither you nor I own the whole world and can never gain such wealth on our own. If God, however, is your Father and you are faithful to Him, then you will inherit all that He wants to give. He owns the whole world, and He will not withhold any good thing from you – if you walk uprightly before Him (Psalm 84:11).

King David is a good example of this. He was a man after God's own heart, who kept God's commandments and followed God with all of his heart, to do what was right in God's eyes (1 King 14:8). Because of this, God promised David that He would establish his son's kingdom forever and that He would be his Father and watch over him. God promised that His mercy would never leave him (2 Samuel 7:12-16).

Even when Solomon turned away from God's ways, God still did not break His promise to David and allowed Solomon to keep his kingdom (1 Kings 11:13). Even though David's son did enough wrong to rightfully allow God to totally cut off his inheritance, God still allowed David's grandson to have part of the kingdom, because of David (1 Kings 11:13).

What God is saying through all of this is that if you really love your children enough to work hard to give them a nice inheritance, then you should work hard at becoming a faithful servant of His, and He will give them more than you would ever be able to give them. So that excuse for saving money is not acceptable in God's eyes.

The worldly man will set aside as large of an amount of money as he can for the future. This is not how a Christian should think. We should live a life of faith in God to meet our every need, as God has promised (Philippians 4:19). We are called to walk by faith and not by sight (2 Corinthians 5:7), and saving our money for our future needs is wrong in God's eyes because we are not trusting Him.

If we say that we have fellowship with Him, and walk in darkness, we lie and do not practice the truth (1 John 1:6). *Now by this we know that we know Him, if we keep His commandments.* (1 John 2:3) *He who says he abides in Him ought himself also to walk just as He walked.* (1 John 2:6)

If we are going to confess Jesus to be Lord of all and tell the world that He is the All-Sufficient One, then we will have to start living it or people won't believe us. Neither will God be able to honor us as He wants to.

I don't totally disagree with saving money to some decree in order to help your children with their college, but I don't agree with saving up all of your life in order to provide them with everything they might need to go to college. In the first place, we don't know how much that will be. In the second place, we don't even know for sure if they are going to go to college. Besides that, they need to be taught responsibility. If they want something, they need to work for it and not always depend on Mom and Dad for everything. College is a good place to start.

As far as that goes, if a Christian feels he needs to save enough to meet certain future needs, he will have the problem of knowing how much is enough. This problem will cause him to forget about God's will and the needs of His kingdom and set his goal toward saving an unlimited amount, which will lead to saving for the rest of his life and, therefore, disqualifying him from being a disciple.

God knows we need a certain amount to meet the needs of our homes, businesses, and personal lives, such as food, clothes, cars, enjoyment, business capital, children's needs, etc., but beyond these necessities Christians should live to further God's Kingdom. Everything over this should go to helping the needy and furthering the Gospel.

A lot of Christians use 2 Corinthians 12:14 as grounds to justify themselves for saving money for their children or their future, instead of using it to further the Gospel, as God has commanded us to. It says: *"For the children ought not to lay up for the parents, but the parents for the children."* But Paul is not talking about a typical household family here.

He is referring to himself as the spiritual parent of the Christians (1 Corinthians 4:14), although natural parents do provide for their children while they are under their care, and not vice versa (at least not until the parents are too old to care for themselves).

Even so, he is not talking about laying up for future or possible future needs; he is talking about immediate needs. Many take this out of context and say it means we should save up for our children's future.

Even here, Paul was not saving anything for his spiritual children. He was helping them with their immediate needs. He fed and nourished them spiritually, to help them find the ways of the Lord, so they could have a future of their own.

As someone once told me, you can give someone a fish and he can eat one time, or you can teach them how to fish, and he can eat for the rest of his life. Paul was able to do this because obedient Christians of other churches were using their money to support him as he spread the Gospel (2 Corinthians 11:7-8).

Another scripture that is used for grounds to justify saving up for the future is 1 Timothy 5:8. It says: *"But if anyone does not provide for his own, and especially for those of his household, he has denied the faith and is worse than an unbeliever."* Here Paul is talking about providing the needs of widows and not children. He isn't saying that we should set them up for the future either. He is saying that we should meet their immediate needs. Their children should do this for them and if they won't, then the church should, and He tells us which widows are eligible (1 Timothy 5:3-16).

God wants us to care for one another in our daily needs. If all Christians obeyed God's Word for what it says and not for what they want it to say, no one would be lacking in their personal lives or ministry.

The Bible uses the ant as an example we should watch and learn from (Proverbs 6:6-8). He tells us how even the ant stores up food for the future. The only problem with the use of this scripture is that the worldly man thinks it means that we should save our wealth for our future on this earth. That is because he is earthly minded and can't see that far into the future.

God is trying to tell us we should store up treasures in Heaven while we have a chance. Once we die, we will have done what we can, as far as for what rewards we will have in Heaven, which is where we will spend eternity.

Where Is Your Heart?

All of our works will be tested by fire, and what wasn't pleasing to God will be burned up (1 Corinthians 3:10-15).

All of the rich people on earth, who think they were wise because they thought they were laying up for their futures, are going to find out that they missed it altogether. They will realize on judgment day that all of what they did was for nothing, but it will be too late.

We brought nothing into this world, and we can't take anything out of it (1 Timothy 6:7). Because they desired to be rich, they fell into a snare which caused their destruction. It is the love of money that is the root of all evil and has caused many to stray from God (1 Timothy 6:9-10).

Many of them will say they weren't in love with money, but that is the snare of the enemy. He doesn't want you to realize your heart is in the wrong place, so he will tell you that you need to save up for future needs.

The truth is that if they were truly in love with God and not themselves and/ or their money, they would have been serving Him instead of themselves and/ or their money. They would have done what He wanted them to do with their life instead of what they wanted or thought they should do with their life.

They would have trusted Him to meet their future needs. We cannot serve God and money (Matthew 6:24) even though some believe they can.

CHAPTER 4

Becoming a Disciple

When I met Jesus, He showed me the truth about myself and life. I saw that almost everything I believed was either wrong or incomplete. When I met Him, I knew at that moment that all of what I had lived for and all of my desires were worthless compared to Him and what He had to offer.

The moment I saw who He was and what He had to offer, I knew I needed it, and I wanted it, so I decided I would do whatever was necessary to get it as the merchant did in Matthew 13:45-46. Jesus is the way, the truth, and the life, and there is no other (John 14:6).

He was offering eternal life (John 3:16) with peace and happiness (Psalm 146:5). He promised that He would meet every need I had (Philippians 4:19) and would give me the desires of my heart (Psalm 37:4). He told me nothing would be impossible for me to do through Him (Philippians 4:13), and that He would never leave me nor forsake me (Hebrews 13:5). He said that He would give me authority over all the power of the enemy and that nothing would hurt me by any means (Luke 10:19).

I asked what I had to do to have this life. He said I would have to make Him Lord of my life, which would mean giving up my old ways, and live in His new ways (Ephesians 4:20-32). I would have to become born all over again (John 3:3-8) by asking Him to be my Lord and then follow Him (Romans 10:9-10), thus making me a child of God.

The wisest thing I ever did was to ask Jesus to become Lord of my life. As time went on, we spent more and more time together. He always took time out for me whenever I wanted Him to. As I got to know Him and saw how beautiful and kind He is, I fell head over heels in love with Him. The more I got to know Him, the more I wanted to serve Him with all of my heart.

I told Him I wanted to follow Him wherever He went, and I was willing to do whatever He wanted me to. I wanted to join His army and be His disciple because He is the King of kings and Lord of lords (Revelation 19:16), and I knew I could totally trust and depend on Him for everything.

Handcuffed to Jesus

Jesus let it be known to me that many are called to follow Him, and I was one of those, but out of the many who are called, only a few will be chosen (Matthew 20:16). The reason few are chosen is because there are many who want the blessings and gifts of God, but the price to have them is higher than most want to pay. So only a few will pay it.

I cried out with all of my heart and told Him that I didn't care what it would cost me. I would pay any price to be His disciple. All I wanted to know is what I had to do and how to do it. I wanted to be one of the few to be chosen.

I knew nothing of this new life. I only knew that Jesus was the most wonderful person I had ever known, and I loved Him with all of my heart. I didn't want to lose Him or His blessings, no matter what the cost.

Becoming a Disciple

I studied the Bible and cried out to Him day and night, day after day, year after year, learning His ways of life and letting Him do whatever it took to change me, so that I would be able to please Him in everything I did (Joshua 1:8). I attended church every chance I had and listened to every sermon I could get my hands on that was preached by a true man of God, in order to renew my mind, so that I could think the way He wanted me to and I could know His perfect will for me (Romans 12:2).

I had a lot of problems in my life and a lot of bad habits, and I knew it wouldn't be easy to overcome some of them. So I had to make up my mind to depend upon God to get me through. Without Him I knew I couldn't do anything (John 15:5).

He told me what to do and how to do it. All I had to do was listen to Him and trust that there was a good reason for Him telling me to make whatever changes I needed to make in order to become the new person.

There were many things that I didn't understand, but the first thing I had to learn is that He is the all-knowing God, and I must trust in Him totally and not lean on my own understandings (Proverbs 3:5). Even when I didn't agree with something He said for me to do, I had to trust and obey Him because His ways and thoughts are so much higher than mine (Isaiah 55:9).

As I grew closer to God, I realized why it is necessary to let go of all of these things in our lives, in order to be His disciple. All He is doing is making us into the image of Jesus (Romans 8:29), who is very unselfish, and though He was in the form of God, came in the form of a bondservant, in the likeness of men (Philippians 2:57).

Becoming a Disciple

If we are to be His disciple, we must be as He is, who was not only a servant, but did only what the Father told Him to do (John 5:30). Besides, the only way we can reap the full blessings is by doing as He pleases.

Because we have chosen Him over our families, homes, lands, and businesses, we will sit on the throne of His glory and receive a hundredfold blessing in return for what we gave up for His name's sake. Though we are counted as last in this world, we will be first in the everlasting world (Matthew 19:27-30).

I began praying to my heavenly Father, asking Him to change my heart. I knew there was no way that I would be able to become as Jesus is on my own, because I was such a wretched sinner, but I also knew that with God nothing is impossible (Luke 1:37). I knew that through Jesus I would be able to do anything (Philippians 4:13).

He told me not to worry about being able to do things right, because I was His workmanship now (Ephesians 2:10), which meant changing me was His problem and not mine. The only thing I had to do was to keep my eyes on Him, follow Him, and trust Him to complete the work. His grace would be sufficient enough to keep me in my weakest moments (2 Corinthians 12:9).

Now that I am His, He will cleanse me from ALL my filthiness, He will take out my hard heart and put in a soft one, and He will put His Spirit within me and cause me to do His will (Ezekiel 36:25-27). He is the Author and the Finisher of my faith (Hebrews 12:2) and not me, therefore, I can trust Him to finish what He started and not have to trust in myself.

60

Becoming a Disciple

I no longer worried about whether I would have a place to sleep, clothes to wear, or food to eat, because Jesus promised me that if I would seek His Kingdom first and His righteousness, He would add all things that I need to my life (Matthew 6:31-34). And He has never let me down. He always hears and answers my prayers.

I remember the day I finally passed my first faith test. I was working as a salesman and was paid strictly on commission. If I didn't sell, I didn't get paid. I liked that kind of a job for several reasons: (1) I could make as much money as I wanted, as long as I made sales, (2) I was an excellent salesman, and (3) God could bless me with as much money as He wanted to, which normally was a good amount.

During this time of testing, I wasn't able to close any sales at all, no matter how hard I tried. All of my money had been used up, and my phone bill was due, which was almost $200.00.

I stood on God's promise that He would meet all of my needs (Philippians 4:19) and held the bill up to Him and said, "God, I need this much money to pay this phone bill. I give this to You and trust in You to take care of it." Then I pinned it up on the bulletin board and forgot about it.

A month passed and another bill came in, so I peeped in the envelope to see how much it was, and it was now close to $300.00. I took the old one off of the bulletin board and threw it in the trash can and put the new one up in its place. At the same time, I said, "God, now I need this much," and I left it there and didn't worry about it. I just trusted Him to take care of it.

Becoming a Disciple

Another month passed and a new bill came in, and now it was a little over $380.00. I took the old one down and threw it in the trash can and put the new one up and told God I now needed that much.

Then it hit me that I was three months behind, owed almost $400.00, and I hadn't even received a late notice. I asked God about it, and He told me that He had blinded the company employees to my being late, because I had trusted Him to take care of it, which meant I didn't insist on Him taking care of it the way I thought He should, but let Him do it His way.

This was really a miracle because everything is computerized, which means He had to stop the computers from picking it up for three months. Because I had totally laid all of my problems on the altar, meaning I gave them to Him, trusting Him to take care of them, He arranged it for me to receive enough money in the mail to pay off the phone bill, car note, insurance, and everything else that was due.

From that moment, my faith soared to the sky, and I have been able to receive His promises as never before and never worry about anything. I knew He would take care of everything, as long as I trusted in, waited on, and obeyed Him in everything.

When I joined His army, I took all of what He said seriously and obeyed Him, because I knew I could trust Him with everything. I knew He wouldn't tell me or any of His children to do anything just to tell us, because He has a reason for everything, and everything that happens is for our good.

In James 1:2-4, the Lord tells us to count it all joy when we go through trials, because our faith is being tested, and through the testing we will learn patience. If we let the testing be completed, trusting in the Lord for the victory and counting it all joy, we will come out perfect, complete, and lacking nothing. So that is what I did, and now I can go anywhere and do anything at anytime that God tells me to and not worry.

Joining the Lord's army is, in many ways, no different from joining the army of your country. One of the similarities is that we must go through a season of training to learn how to properly fight against our enemies. Unfortunately, the Church is the only army that takes in recruits and sends them out to do battle unprepared. That is why so many Christians go out to tell the world about Jesus and get beat up, wounded, and discouraged physically, emotionally, and spiritually and don't want to go out again. We need to take time out to train God's people to use the weapons He gave us outside of regular church services. Satan is having a ball with Christians who were told they have power over all evil, but haven't been shown or taught how to use this power.

When you join the military, they don't just give you a rifle and a box of bullets and send you out into battle. They don't spend only a few hours a week training their soldiers to fight and then send them out to war. They have training classes, special training classes and special-special training classes, in order to train soldiers to fight and win. The Lord's army should be trained the same way – TO WIN.

CHAPTER 5

Forsaking All

So likewise, whoever of you does not forsake all that he has cannot be My disciple.   Luke 14:33

In order to be a disciple of Jesus, you must forsake ALL that doesn't represent Him. No one can be His disciple unless they put Him first above all other things in their lives. He is a jealous God (Deuteronomy 6:15) and doesn't want any halfhearted children (Revelation 3:16).

His first command is to love Him with ALL of your heart, soul, mind, and strength (Mark 12:30). This means that He is not interested in you loving Him whenever you feel like it, or even sharing his throne in your life with anyone or anything else. He is a jealous God and will not allow anything to sit on the throne with Him (Deuteronomy 6:14-15). He must have total authority in your life, or He isn't your Lord.

If we ask Him to be Lord of our lives, then we had better take Him seriously and give Him the throne. If it wasn't that serious, then He would not have made it His first command.

Being lord of anything means to have total lordship or authority over everything involved with it. If we confess Jesus as our Lord but won't give Him complete control of our lives, then that only makes us a hypocrite. We are saying that Jesus is Lord, but we are still making all of our own choices, instead of obeying what He tells us to do. To put it simply, we are being lord of our lives, instead of Him.

He is not a dictator, but He does need our permission to guide, protect, bless, and provide everything we need in our lives. As a young child, our parents had complete authority over our lives … until we were old enough to make wise decisions for ourselves. In the same way, our heavenly Father wants to teach us to make wise decisions, according to His eternal and supernatural Kingdom, so we will be able to be safe and successful in all His ways.

At first I wasn't sure if He really meant we had to actually forsake ALL, but as I got to know Him, I realized that He literally meant ALL or He would not have said it. Jesus is very firm in what

He says. He is the truth (John 14:6) and will not lie or exaggerate. He means what He says and says what He means, though most people have a hard time believing and accepting that.

He did not say *some* would have to forsake all to be His disciple. He said, "... *WHOEVER OF YOU* ... , " which means everyone, with no exceptions.

He did not say we could just *say* we would forsake all with or without the intention of actually doing it, or that we just had to be willing to forsake all, justifying our disobedience by saying, "He knows my heart." No, He said, "... *WHOEVER OF YOU DOES NOT FORSAKE ALL ...*"

He did not say that we could forsake only a part and still be His disciple. He said "... *WHOEVER OF YOU DOES NOT FORSAKE ALL THAT HE HAS ...*"

He did not say that we would be able to partly be His disciple, if we hung on to some things and forsook some things. He said, "... *CANNOT BE MY DISCIPLE...*"

As I earnestly sought for the true meaning of forsaking ALL, I learned that He meant that we had to let go of all material possessions, desires, and relationships that were not necessary in life and/or edifying to us as a Christian, glorifying His name, and use whatever we had over our needs to further His Kingdom.

His will being done must be more important than our own selfish desires. If any plans or desires of ours would prevent or even stand in the way of immediate obedience to His commands, we must push them aside and follow Him, or we will miss our calling.

In Luke 9:59-62, we read about two men who were given a choice of forsaking all to follow Jesus or miss their opportunity to serve God. In verses 59-60, Jesus called a man to follow Him, but the man wanted to first go and bury his dead father (or wait until he died before following Him). Jesus told him to let the dead bury the dead and for him to come now.

There is nothing wrong or immoral about anyone wanting to bury their dead relatives, but Jesus told him to make his choice. Evidently he wanted to bury his father more than he wanted to follow Jesus, because not only was he left nameless, but we never hear of him again.

In verses 61-62, we read about another who voluntarily offered to follow Jesus, but first he wanted to go and tell his family good-bye. Here Jesus told him that he could come, but he must come right then and not look back. This man also missed his chance to walk with Jesus or we would have heard more about him.

Simon called Peter and Andrew his brother, along with the rest of the twelve disciples who walked with Jesus, set good examples of forsaking all at the moment Jesus called them. They were fisherman, casting their nets to catch food when their call came, and yet they immediately left their nets where they were and followed Jesus, with no questions asked (Matthew 4:18-20).

James and John were also fisherman and were in their boat with their father mending their nets when Jesus called them. They also immediately left their father, the boat and their nets, with no questions asked and went with Jesus (Matthew 4:21-22). I can imagine the look on their father's face as they suddenly got up and left him and their livelihood to follow Jesus.

They didn't sit and discuss it with their parents, only to come back and tell Jesus, "I'm sorry, Jesus, but I can't go right now. My family doesn't understand, so I need to stay with them for now. I thank You for asking me, but it's just a bad time. Maybe another time. I know You will understand because You are a forgiving and understanding God."

Jesus might be a forgiving and understanding God, but He is God and when He speaks, He expects us to obey. If we don't, then we will be the ones to lose our blessings, and someone else will get them, because He will find someone who will obey Him.

I remember when God called me to drop everything and follow Him. I was vice president of a company, had a nice car that wasn't totally paid for, and two trained guard dogs, one of them as close to me as my own family and was valued at around $1,000. Normally there was no way I would even consider parting with them. But God spoke to me and said "Guy, I am calling you again. You can either come now or stay where you are, and I'll get someone else." I immediately resigned from my job, sold my car for enough to pay it off, found a good home for my dogs and gave them away, and hopped on the bus and went where He told me to go.

Being a disciple of Christ places high demands on us, and few are willing to pay the price. Of course, few are bright enough to plan that far ahead. All they see is what life on earth has to offer and they never think about the real retirement.

Most people won't let go of anything that they enjoy having for themselves, even if God tells them to do it. They don't realize that when they gave their life to Jesus, they became His and are no longer their own. They were bought with a price, and therefore should give the Owner authority over His property (1 Corinthians 6:19-20).

At first, it seemed to me as though the life of a disciple of Christ would be very unfulfilling. The reason for that was because I had always been a very selfish person. I thought of myself as unselfish, because many times I would give to others and do things to help those in need, which always made me feel good about myself.

When I made Jesus Lord of my life, before I would give something away, I began asking Him if it was His will for me to give anything to anyone or help anyone in any way that I thought I should. By doing this, I was able to still help people, but I was able to please

Forsaking All

God at the same time. If He told me not to give or help, I knew there was a good reason, and I obeyed Him.

Now that I am doing things His way, I am storing up treasure in Heaven because on Judgment Day all of our works will be tested by fire. Only those that were done in His will are going to remain with us (1 Corinthians 3:10-15).

CHAPTER 6

Denying Self

Then Jesus said to His disciples, If anyone desires to come after Me, let him deny himself, and take up his cross, and follow Me. Matthew 16:24

If we want to be His disciple and follow after Him, we will have to deny ourselves. In order to be able to deny self the way He meant, we must give Jesus total lordship of our entire life.

We have been bought with a price

and therefore are no longer our own (1 Corinthians 6:19-20). We belong to the One who bought us, therefore, we have no right to say what we will have, say, or do with our lives.

As disciples of Christ, we must truly give all of our rights to God, which means that we will have no will of our own outside of doing His will. Just as Paul, we will become prisoners of our Lord (Ephesians 4:1). We will spend every moment in the attitude of prayer (1 Thessalonians 5:17) to know what He wants us to do and say in all situations.

No matter what happens, we know that He is in charge of all things, and nothing can happen unless He allows it to happen (Matthew 10:28-31). Therefore, we give thanks to Him for all things, whether good or bad (1 Thessalonians 5:18). All we want is to please Him. Every move we make, every breath we take we pray will be pleasing to Him.

We have fallen so in love with Him that we can't get Him out of our heart. We wake up with Him on our mind, and He stays there until we go to sleep. We dream of Him through the night. We eat, drink, and breathe Jesus because He is the most wonderful Person we have ever known. He died for us (Romans 5:8), therefore, we will live for Him.

Denying ourselves wasn't that hard of a decision because we are naturally willing to do anything that will bring us great rewards and happiness. By denying ourselves, we not only get the honor of personally walking and talking with God, just as Adam and Eve did, but we get unspeakable joy (1 Peter 1:8) and eternal rewards that no man or circumstances can steal. They will never rust, rot, or fade away (Matthew 6:20).

Denying Self

Denying self isn't the same as self-denial. Self-denial is when you do without certain foods, not doing things you enjoy, or not having materialistic things that you desire. Denying self is to remove self from all authority in your life and giving it to Jesus. Our life belongs to Him, and we must be led by His Spirit in all things. Many people get these two confused and miss the mark of becoming a true disciple.

Self-denial, however, does play an important part in our spiritual growth because it teaches us self-control. Fasting from food, TV, or any other events that the flesh loves to do is self-denial. As long as you are doing it as a sacrifice to move God and replace it with prayer or the Word of God, you will be crucifying the flesh and learning self-control.

A eunuch for Jesus is a good example of a true disciple. A eunuch in the

Old Testament was a man who was so in love with the king that he would do anything for him. He was a man whom the king had to be able to totally trust because he watched over the queen and her valuables while the king was away. His life was nothing but a desire to please the king in everything he did.

Eunuchs would protect the king's bride, feed her, watch over her as she slept, carry heavy things for her, and even help her get dressed when needed. The king had to be able to totally trust him with his wives while he was away, so they would castrate him. This way the king knew the guard couldn't have sex with his wives, because he wasn't physically able.

According to Matthew 19:12, there are three kinds of eunuchs. (1) Some men were born that way, meaning that they were deformed and/or for some other reason couldn't perform sexually. (2) Some were made that way by man. These were prisoners of war who were selected and forced to become eunuchs. (3) The third kind of eunuchs were those who volunteered to have the operation out of devotion in order to serve the king where he needed them. Some of them had been married, but had lost their wife through death, and having no wife, they chose to become a eunuch.

This third kind, a eunuch by his own choice, is the one who was a true disciple. He wasn't a eunuch because he was born that way and, therefore, had no choice in the matter. He wasn't forced by circumstances or men to devote his life to serving the king. Rather, he loved the king so much that he chose to sacrifice his life to serve, seeking no personal pleasures of his own, to care for the king's bride.

A true disciple of Christ is of the same devotion. He loves the King of kings so much that he chooses to sacrifice his life to take care of the King's affairs and the King's bride, which is the Church. He will watch over the members of the Church, feed them, clothe them, and do all that is necessary to prepare the Bride for the King's return, seeking no pleasure for himself. Although he will have much treasure stored up for him by doing so (Luke 12:42-44), he will not be doing it for the treasure, but only to please the King.

God gives a warning to those who tend to His people for selfish gain and don't take care of them as a true shepherd should (Ezekiel 34:1-10). God is looking for true eunuchs that He can trust with His treasures.

Denying self the way Jesus is speaking of is to give up all of your personal pleasures and desires and live to please

My Testimony

Him. I remember when I had a problem with watching TV and God wanted me to spend time with Him, so He could tell me something. I didn't have a problem with watching ungodly shows or not being able to tear myself away from the TV, as a matter of fact I watched very little TV. I would only watch an hour to an hour and a half of simple, old time, comedy shows, and this was done in the later evening hours, to try to unwind and take my mind off of my daily struggles.

I wrestled with God for the longest time about those few moments, which I took to myself to enjoy my time. "There is nothing wrong with what I am doing," I kept telling Him and myself. I would keep bringing up the fact that I would spend all day, every day, doing anything He wanted me to, and I thought I deserved this time to do what I wanted.

God let me go as I pleased, because He won't force us to do anything against our will, but I was miserable because I loved Him so much, and I knew it was hurting Him when I would ignore Him. All He wanted to do was to spend some time with me, bless me, and love me.

I could have gone on for the rest of my life doing as self wanted to do, but I would have missed the rewards God had for me. When I finally realized I really needed to turn the TV off and go and spend that time with Him, I chose to do it.

The only problem was that self didn't want to do it, and now that I had decided to do it, I had to battle with that old rebellious nature of mine. In every battle, there is one winner and one loser, so I sat down and examined the whole situation and weighed both sides out to see what the wisest thing to do would be.

Denying Self

On one side I could give into self and watch TV trying to get some pleasure out of life and miss out on what God wanted to give me (which is always better than anything the world has to offer). On the other side I could spend time with God and truly get filled with His awesome presence, but I would have to fight with the desire of self and the temptation of watching TV.

As time went on, I stopped watching TV during those times that God wanted to spend time with me. As I spent time with God, I realized that He gave me more pleasure and satisfaction than any TV program did. At the same time, I would get closer to Him and learn more about Him and what He had in store for me.

Realizing this, I could see that every moment spent with God was the wisest and most fulfilling way I could spend my time. So I decided to get rid of the TV altogether. That way not only would I not be tempted to go back to it, but I would find true happiness and contentment by letting God be my TV. I denied self by giving God my right to have and watch TV and made Him Lord of that area also.

Now that I have given my right to Him, He has the say so of whether or not I will watch or have a TV. As with everything else, when we give our rights to God, it doesn't mean that we will never be able to do those things again. It means that He will decide the matter.

When we are mature enough and have self-control over the situation, God will give the right back to us. The only difference is that it won't be a right anymore. It will now be a privilege, and we will appreciate it and won't abuse it.

Since I have done that, I have found such an excellent peace and total fulfillment in my life, just as He said I would. He is worth every moment I have to give to Him.

I remember being head over heels in love with my high school sweetheart. It seemed that there wasn't enough time in the day, because every moment away from her was filled with nothing but daydreams of being with her again. I thought of nothing but her and what I could do to make her happy.

She brought such joy to my heart that I felt like I was on clouds, just thinking about her. Since I have given up TV and started spending my time with God, I have fallen head over heels in love with Him, and He gives me the same fulfillment, only better. We must be willing to do whatever we have to do in order to let Him truly be Lord of our lives.

The Bible tells us to remove from our lives whatever causes us to sin (Mark 9:43-47). The sin that I was committing was not going to send me to Hell, but the principle behind these scriptures applies here also. I was not loving God with all of my heart, soul, mind, and strength (Mark 12:30), because there were still those moments when the TV had control of me and not God. In that aspect, it is sin (James 4: 17), and it would have robbed me of a blessing.

These are the end times, the last of the last days, and there will be no more eunuchs by birth, as John the Baptist was. God isn't looking for eunuchs who were made that way through circumstances either. The ones He will allow to be an eunuch are those who choose to be that way because they love Him. These are the ones He knows He can trust with

Denying Self

His Bride (who is the Church), while He is away.

In Old Testament times, it actually took an operation to meet the requirements for becoming a eunuch. In the New Testament, it simply takes a commitment to serve and love the Lord with all of your heart, soul, mind, and strength.

God doesn't care how old you are or how much sin you have committed in your life. He doesn't care if you are married, single, or divorced. All He cares about is truly being your Lord. You can start whenever, wherever, and whoever you are, but if you don't – you CANNOT be His disciple.

CHAPTER 7

Taking Up Our Cross

Then Jesus said to His disciples, "If anyone desires to come after Me, let him deny himself, and take up his cross, and follow Me." Matthew 16:24

We also have to choose to take up our cross, which means that things will happen to us that would appear dishonorable in the eyes of the world. The cross stands for the abuse, persecution, and shame that Jesus went through, which means that those who choose to take up their cross will also go through some of the same.

Years ago the Romans used the cross as a means of executing and torturing criminals and rebellious people. After Emperor Constantine became a Christian, the use of the cross in execution and torture ceased, and the people looked at the cross as a sacred symbol, because Jesus had died on one.

Although people have carried the cross as a symbol of Christianity to this day, we must not let it have any more meaning in our souls than what it really is – a symbol. Many people cling to the cross as much as they do to Jesus, and that is a form of idolatry.

The truth of it is that Jesus represents life, and the cross represents death. Because the cross does represent death, some believe that taking up our cross means dying to the flesh or the sinful desires of man. This isn't what the Bible is referring to when it talks about Jesus dying the death of the cross (Philippians 2:8).

The death of the cross was the horrible death of torture that Jesus went through for us on the cross. The Bible even tells us in Galatians 3:13 that anyone hung from a tree is cursed. The tree it is talking about, in Jesus' case, was the wooden cross.

Truly taking up our cross in the manor Jesus is speaking of means that we will be persecuted, ridiculed, slandered, jailed, beaten, and at times even killed going into dangerous areas to tell the lost and confused about Jesus and His promise of salvation. We are unable to hold certain jobs and, at times, even lose the ones we have – if the job included some involvement with ungodly activity such as selling liquor, cigarettes, lottery tickets, etc. It would come to a point of choosing to either continue in the straight and narrow path of righteousness with Jesus or give into man's way of doing things.

There are many examples of true men of God in the Bible who took up their cross and suffered verbal abuse and physical harm. Jesus warned us that the world would hate us because they first hated Him. He chose us out of the world, therefore, we represent Him (John 15:18-19) and all that He stands for.

Jesus exposed the sinful ways of men, and therefore, they have no excuse to continue in sin, and they hate Him because of it (John 15:22-24). Since we have taken up our cross and are following Him, meaning we are doing as He did, the world will hate us also and do to us as they did to Him, all because they do not know God (John 15:21).

The Bible tells us, in Acts 7:51-60, about Stephen, who was a great man of God and continued in the ways of the Lord by speaking the truth to all who would listen. He told the unbelievers that they were being rebellious to the Holy Spirit, just as their fathers had been. They persecuted the prophets and killed those who told of the coming of Jesus (v. 51 -53).

When the people heard Stephen, they were furious because he was speaking the truth. At that moment, being filled with the Holy Spirit, Stephen looked up to Heaven and saw the glory of God and Jesus standing at the right hand of God, and said, *"Look! I see the Heavens opened and the Son of Man standing at the right hand of God!"* (v. 54-56).

Then they cried out with a loud voice, stopped their ears, and all ran after him at the same time. They grabbed him, threw him out of the city, and stoned him to death. As they were stoning him, he looked up to Heaven and asked God to receive him. Then he as Jesus had done, by asking God to forgive them (v. 57-60).

Isaiah was a prophet who did and said what God told him to and was sawed in two because of it. Others had trials of mocking and scourging, chains and imprisonment, were tempted, and slain with the sword. They wandered about in sheepskins and goatskins, being destitute, afflicted, tormented. They wandered in deserts and mountains, in dens and caves of the earth (Hebrews 11:36-38). They didn't go through these tribulations because they had no choice, but because they chose to. They could have used the power God had given them, but they didn't accept deliverance, so that they would obtain a better resurrection (Hebrews 11:35). This is what Christ did for us, and they were following Him.

Jesus died for all, that those who live should no longer live for themselves, but for Him (2 Corinthians 5:15). As children of Christ, we must suffer with Him in order to inherit with Him and be glorified with Him (Romans 8:16-17). If we are not suffering for Him and aren't willing to suffer for Him, then we need to ask ourselves whether or not He is really our Lord. Most will realize that Jesus is just a Savior to them and not their Lord.

All who desire to live godly in Christ Jesus will suffer persecution (2 Timothy 3:12). It is a privilege and an honor to suffer for His name sake, and this privilege has been given to us by God Himself (Philippians 1:29).

Just as Jesus learned obedience by the things He suffered (Hebrews 5:8), we also will learn obedience by the things we suffer. If we suffer because of the good we are doing in His name and take it patiently, our suffering will be commendable before God (1 Peter 2:20).

Christ suffered for us, and we are to have the same mind as Him and follow His example by living the rest of our lives to fulfill the will of God (1 Peter 4:1). Christ suffered for us, and we are called to follow His steps and suffer for others (1 Peter 2:21).

We are commanded to love our neighbor as ourselves (Mark 12:31), and we do this by laying our lives down for the brethren (1 John 3: 16). We suffer for three reasons. (1) To learn obedience,

(2) For the benefit of others whom we can help through their struggles (2 Corinthians 1:3-8) and (3) To come to know Him and be as His (Philippians 3:7-14).

Paul was called of God just as we are. He was shown how many things he was to suffer for Jesus' sake (Acts 9: 16) and because of his love for God, he endured to the end and finished the race he was running (2 Timothy 4:7).

Paul was whipped thirty-nine lashes five times, stoned and left for dead, shipwrecked, thrown in prison, beaten with rods three times, and robbed and he suffered many other things (2 Corinthians 11:23-28). It is hard to say that suffering for the Lord's sake isn't of God when God used Paul to write most of the New Testament.

The apostles were beaten and commanded not to speak in the name of Jesus by the authorities. Because of this, they walked away rejoicing that they were counted worthy to suffer shame for His name (Acts 5:40-42). They were used by God as a spectacle to the world, both to angels and to men (1 Corinthians 4:9-13).

As disciples of Christ, we must accept the wrong done to us and let ourselves be defrauded (1 Corinthians 6:7). We do not fear what man can do to us because he can only kill the body and not the soul. Instead, we fear God, who can destroy both soul and body in Hell (Matthew 10:28).

We are not afraid of losing what we have in God and so we suffer these things, knowing that God is able to keep what we have committed to Him until that Day (2 Timothy 1:12). If we endure to the end, we shall reign with Him (2 Timothy 2:12).

Those who don't believe it is good to suffer for the Lord's name sake don't know Him. Those who confess to know Him but aren't willing to suffer for Him and their brethren are rebellious to God and don't love Him (John 14:15).

To know the Lord means that you have an intimate relationship with Him, just as a husband and wife know one another because they have an intimate relationship with each other. You can know *of* Him by hearing and reading all about Him, just as you can know *of* George Washington by hearing and reading all about him. But, unless you have a personal relationship with Him, you will not know Him.

Not everyone who says to Me, "Lord, Lord," shall enter the kingdom of heaven, but he who does the will of My Father in heaven. Many will say to Me in that day, "Lord, Lord, have we not prophesied in Your name, cast out demons in

Taking Up Our Cross

Your name, and done many wonders in Your name?" And then I will declare to them, "I never knew you; depart from Me, you who practice lawlessness!"

Matthew 7:21-23

CHAPTER 8

Following Jesus

Then Jesus said to His disciples, "If anyone desires to come after Me, let him deny himself, and take up his cross, and follow Me." Matthew 16:24

Along with denying ourselves and taking up our cross, we have to choose to follow Jesus. Following Him means that we will go where He tells us to go, do what He tells us to do, and say what He tells us to say. We must do His will when He tells us to do it and do it the way He tells us to do it and not the way we think would be best.

We live as a servant of the most high God by serving others and walking in the power and might of the Holy Spirit. No matter what anyone does or says to us that is wrong, we do our best to be patient, longsuffering, and forgiving, walking in the love of Christ, or we will be as nothing (1 Corinthians 13:1-7). Although many times the challenge is stronger than we are able to handle and we fall short of God's glory (Romans 3:23), we are covered by His grace (2 Corinthians 12:9).

Our life is a life of zeal for God's will to be done. We strive to master the flesh, consistently show the full power of the nine gifts of the Holy Spirit (1 Corinthians 12:7-11), and the fruits of the Holy Spirit, which are love, joy, peace, longsuffering, kindness, goodness, faithfulness, gentleness, and self-control (Galatians 5:22-23). Our desire is to walk as Jesus walked and bear much fruit, that we will glorify our Father and be His disciple (John 15:8).

The world looks at this as being in bondage and having to do whatever we are told, with no choice of our own. They don't want to follow Jesus because they believe that it is a dreadful life and one in which they won't be able to do anything they enjoy. This is a total deception from Satan. Following Jesus is a life full of joy and peace. We don't care about the things we can't do.

We don't have time to think about all of the things that our Lord doesn't want us to do. We are so in love with Him that we spend all of our time asking Him what we can do for Him. Our whole life revolves around doing all that we can to please Him.

IF ANYONE COMES TO ME AND DOES NOT HATE HIS FATHER AND MOTHER, WIFE AND CHIL- DREN, BROTHERS AND SISTERS, YES, AND HIS OWN LIFE ALSO, HE CANNOT BE MY DISCIPLE.
Luke 14:26

Now, He didn't mean that we should literally hate them or even have any ill feelings of any kind toward them. What He meant was that if we wanted to be His disciple we would have to be so in love with Him that our love for our family or ourselves would not be able to sway us in the least from doing His will instead of theirs or our own. We are to love them as we love ourselves, but not as we love Jesus.

Many times we will have to choose between doing what someone in the family or we ourselves want us to do and doing what God wants us to do. If what they or we want to do is not in God's perfect will, we must choose not to participate.

Others may not see any harm in doing what they want us to do. But because we have obeyed God and studied His Word intensely, as He has instructed us to do, so that we may rightly divide the Word of truth (2 Timothy 2:15), we know what His perfect will allows us to do and not do. If we know it is wrong and we do it anyway, then to us it will be sin (James 4:17).

Jesus said that if we abide in His Word, meaning to live by it, then we are His disciples (John 8:31). If we live by His Word, we will know the truth, and the truth will make us free (John

8:32). The reason so many people think they are living right, when they really aren't, is because they haven't taken the time to find out what the true will of God is.

When most people are told that they are sinning in some area of their life, they reject it, because they love themselves and their sin more than they love Jesus. Jesus tells us that if we love Him, we will obey His commandments (John 14:15). This means that if we won't obey His commandments, then we really don't love Him.

If we don't lay aside all sinful ways and start doing what God's Word tells us to do, instead of just hearing what it tells us to do, we will be deceiving ourselves into believing that we are doing right, when we are really doing wrong, and God's blessings won't be with us as He wants them to be (James 1:21-25).

Handcuffed to Jesus

Because of being deceived in truth, many times our families and friends will want us to participate in some event that seems innocent to them. And when we won't participate in something because we know that it is sin in the eyes of God, they can't accept that fact. Often they won't even accept the fact that it is sin or even be willing to look at what the Bible says about it. If they did, they would find out that they must change, and they don't want to (Matthew 13:15). This is true of most people in the world.

Many times we even lose fellowship with our own families and friends because they get very offended at us when we won't give in to the ways of the world, or fellowship with any ways of darkness, because God commands us not to (Ephesians 5:11). We love God and, therefore, choose to obey His commandments (John 14:15) over all others.

Following Jesus

Jesus said that He didn't come to bring peace but division between those who believe in Him and those who don't (Matthew 10:34-36). He came to separate good from evil. Because good and evil don't mix, family and friends will either choose to stay away from us, or if their sinful ways are bad enough, we will have to choose to separate from them, for our Lord's name sake, as well as our own good.

Because some will follow Jesus and some won't, houses will be divided, father against son, and son against father, mother against daughter, and daughter against mother, mother-in-law against daughter-in-law, and daughter-in-law against mother-in-law (Luke 12:51-53).

God does command us to honor our father and mother. This is the first commandment, with the promise that it will be well with us, and we may live long on the earth (Ephesians 6:2-3).

In order to keep the meaning of this scripture in true context with God's will, we must consider that the word *honor* doesn't necessarily mean "to obey." We are to listen to what our parents have to say, take it into consideration, and compare it to the perfect will of God, before rejecting it. We honor them by showing them respect, taking care of them when they are no longer able to take care of themselves, and doing what we can to help them, etc. (Proverbs 23:22). But when they want us to do something that is contrary to God's Word, then we must choose to serve God instead.

This applies to those who are mature enough to know the right way to go and not to those who are still under the dependency of their parents support. If we are still living under their roof, then we need to follow the rules of their house, or we will be in rebellion. If we are still under their care, then we are commanded by God to obey them in all things, for this is well pleasing to the Lord (Colossians 3:20).

If the rules are wrong, by being against God's will, then we will have to look at the consequences of doing what we feel God wants us to do and decide what is the right thing to do in God's eyes. But if we feel a rule is wrong simply because it is against our own will or opinion, then we need to submit to it.

At the same time, however, if we choose to go against the rules of the house, because we believe they are sin and we want to serve God, we must remain open to the Holy Spirit with a teachable attitude, so He can correct us through our parents or any other source. If we don't do this, then we are serving self instead of God, and God won't honor our decision, because it is nothing but rebellion, which is as the sin of witchcraft (1 Samuel 1 5:23).

The second commandment of the Lord is that we must love others as we love ourselves (Mark 12:31). Instead of being selfish and greedy, we must walk in the image of Jesus, who died to meet the needs of others. If we have something and see a brother in need, we will give it to him, because the love of God is in us (1 John 3:17).

All will know that we are disciples of Jesus, if we love one another as Jesus loved us (John 13:34-35). This kind of love is unconditional. It doesn't take offense to what anyone does or doesn't do that doesn't seem right. Instead of taking things personally that are wrongfully done and getting offended, we hope the best for them and love them (1 Corinthians 13:4-8).

There are times when we are made as uncomfortable as possible by man and Satan, but we continue on knowing that our Lord is with us and will keep us (2 Timothy 1:12). We must love our enemies, do good to those who hate us, bless those who curse us, and pray for those who spitefully use us (Luke 6:27-28).

Sometimes we don't know where we will sleep or eat next, because we have chosen to live as Jesus lives, which is to do the will of our heavenly Father. If God should tell us to pack up and go somewhere to serve Him, then we need to go with no questions asked. When we pray the Lord's Prayer, and pray that His will be done on earth as it is in Heaven, we mean it from our hearts and not just our lips.

Jesus did not consider any place on earth to be His home. His home was and is in Heaven. Although we are in the world, we are not of the world (John 17: 14). We are only passing through, being prepared by God to serve Him forever in Heaven (1 Chronicles 29:15 and Hebrews 11:13).

Jesus was constantly doing the will of His Father (Luke 2:49) and didn't know where He was going to be from one day to the next. That is what Jesus meant when He said, *"Foxes have holes, and birds of the air have nests, but the Son of Man has nowhere to lay His head"* (Luke 9:58).

Not only are we not our own, but nothing on earth or in Heaven is ours to do with it as we please. It all belongs to God. He is in control of all things, and we give thanks to Him for all that we have, because He is the one who allowed us to have it (1 Chronicles 29:11-13).

We want to be good stewards of what He gave us, so we use it to further His Kingdom instead of our own. God is faithful, however, to always provide what we need.

God has entrusted us with His power to rule over evil (Luke 10: 19) and has blessed us with all that we need. All of us will give an account to God Himself for what we have or have not done with these gifts while we are on this earth (Luke 12:42-48).

Many times it would be much easier to just throw in the towel and quit, but we must keep on going. No matter how tough things seem to be, our faith and love for Jesus keeps us looking ahead and going forward. Anyone who begins serving God and looks back is not fit for the Kingdom of God (Luke 9:62).

CHAPTER 9

What Is True Love?

BY THIS ALL WILL KNOW THAT YOU ARE MY DISCIPLES, IF YOU HAVE LOVE FOR ONE ANOTHER.

John 13:35

Love is the key to all things that are good and of God. God is love (1 John 4:8), and all good things come from Him (James 1:17). We can have all the money in the world, own everything a person could want, and move in all of the power and gifts of God, but if we don't have love, we are nothing. If we give all of our life and money to helping the poor and don't have love, we will profit nothing (1 Corinthians 13:1-3).

There are three kinds of love described in the Greek. (1) *Eros,* which is a physical and/or sexual drive. (2) *Phileo,* which is an affectionate or emotional love and goes no deeper than the psychological part of man, and (3) *Agape,* which is the unconditional love of God Who loves and accepts us just as we are, regardless of what we do or don't do. This is true love. True love is when we love others because we want to and not because they deserve it or because we want something from them. If we love only those who love us, do good only to those who do good to us, or lend to others only to receive something back, we will profit nothing from God (Luke

6:32-34) because what we do won't be done out of love. It will be done out of selfishness and greed.

Love comes by choice, just as hate does. God loves us unconditionally and has shown us this by giving His only begotten Son, to be sacrificed, in order that we might be forgiven for all our sins and so that we could be able to be with Him throughout eternity (John 3:16). He loves us as much as He loves Himself (John 17:23).

Christ loves us so much that He gave Himself as an offering and a sacrifice for us (Ephesians 5 :2), and He commands us to love one another as He has loved us. Just as He laid His life down for us, we are to lay our lives down for our friends (John 15:12-13).

When you truly love someone, you will be very patient with them when they can't or don't do something right.

What Is True Love?

If they do something wrong, true love for them will enable you to do your best to treat them with kindness and love them into doing it right, instead of getting frustrated and saying or doing something that will only make matters worse.

If you truly love others, you won't be jealous or envious over happy, successful, or prosperous events in their lives. Instead, you will rejoice with them and be happy that they were blessed, wishing more blessings on them, because love is never selfish. Instead of being joyful from having things your way, your joy will come from seeing others with what makes them happy.

When you have love in your heart for others, you will do your best to never allow pride to come in and cause you to boast about yourself to others. You will strive to not say or do any rude thing that would bring jealousy or offense in another's heart by showing contempt for others.

True love will cause you to forgive everyone for all wrong done to you and accept others just as they are, in spite of anything in their lives. When someone gets in trouble for something they did to you or anyone else that was wrong, you will be happy that truth has won, and they can be helped, instead of rejoicing over the fact that they are in trouble.

When you love someone, you will always stick by their side and defend them, even when they make a mistake or do something wrong. You will remain loyal – no matter what the cost.

You will always believe in them and expect the best of them, no matter how many times they mess up. Love is perfect and goes on forever (1 Corinthians 13:4-8).

What Is True Love?

This type of love can only be given through having the love of God in us. We must love Him in order to have His love in us. If we do love Him, then we will keep His commandments (John 14:15).

By keeping His commandments, we will know that we know Him. If we say that we know Him, but we don't keep His commandments, then we are a liar, because the truth is not in us. Whoever keeps His Word has the perfected love of God in them. If we say we keep His commandments, then we should walk just as He walked (1 John 2:3-6).

Few people will make it to Heaven (Matthew 7:14). Of those who do make it, few will become disciples because their heart is in the wrong place. God has instructed us not to love the world or the things in the world. If anyone loves the world, the love of the Father is not in him (1 John 2: 15).

If we have a desire for worldly things, whether it be immorality, riches, or wanting something to make us feel or look worthy (pride), then we are not living for God, because He is not involved in those things (1 John 2:16).

The only way we will be able to love others with a pure *agape* love, as God has commanded us to, is if we become as Christ in thought and deed. He made Himself of no reputation and took on the form of a servant (Philippians 2:5-7), just as we should do.

Just as He did, we also must do nothing for self gain in any form or fashion. We must be a servant to all, by esteeming others better than ourselves, and look out for their interest, as well as our own (Philippians 2:3-4).

The second greatest commandment of the Lord is to love your neighbor as yourself (Mark 12:31). He didn't say to only love the nice neighbor; He said "neighbor," which means all neighbors, whether good or bad.

Jesus instructed us to love our enemies, do good to those who hate us, bless those who curse us, and pray for those who spitefully use us. If someone strikes us on one cheek, we are to offer the other also, and if someone steals our cloak, we should give him our tunic also (Luke 6:27-29).

In the movie *Les Misérables,* a priest offers a homeless convict something to eat from his church. While the priest goes to the back of the church to get the food, the convict grabs a silver candlestick holder and runs out the door in search of a place to sell it.

The police see him running away and stop him. When they see the candlestick holder, they ask the man where he got it. He says the priest gave it to

him. They don't believe him, so they
bring him back to the church and ask
the priest.

When the policeman tells the man
of God what the homeless convict has
claimed, he can tell them the truth, and
they will arrest the convict and return
the candlestick holder. Instead, the
priest looks at the poor man and says,
"Oh, yes, but you forgot something."
And, with this, he hands the convict the
matching silver candlestick holder.

At first, the convict just looks at the
priest in amazement, but then, overcome by this act of selfless love, he begins to weep and ends up giving his life
to the Lord. That was a true depiction
of what a man of God should be and
how the love of God should work.

Through the love, forgiveness, and
acceptance of the priest, that lost man
became a Christian and started serving

the Lord. The value of the man's soul was of greater value than the candlestick holders to the man of God.

One of the greatest examples of God's love is given in the Bible through Hosea. The name *Hosea* means "salvation," and as we read through the book of Hosea, we see a magnificent example of the love of Jesus. Let's begin at chapter 1 and go through chapter 3.

God told Hosea to marry a harlot and have children by (1:2). Hosea married the harlot, whose name was Gomer, and she bore him a son (1:3). The Lord told Hosea to name him *Jezreel*, which stood for the great slaughter that God would bring upon the house of Jehu for the bloodshed he had caused in the city of Jezreel (1:4).

Then Gomer bore a daughter, and the Lord said to call her *Lo-ruhamah* (1:6), which meant "not pitied," and stood for God's anger toward Israel, meaning that He would have no more mercy on them.

Gomer then bore another son, and God said to call him *Lo-ammi*, meaning "not mine," which stood for God's rejection of the people of Israel (1:8-9). He disowned them because of their rebellion and unfaithfulness. It also meant that the child was not for Hosea.

God told Hosea to marry this harlot to show how His children had been unfaithful to Him by worshiping false gods (1:2). Just as Israel had left God, Gomer left Hosea and their children to return to prostitution. Just as God's love never dies, Hosea never stopped loving Gomer.

Although Gomer left her home, children, and the comforts Hosea had provided for her to commit adultery with other men, God told Hosea to go after her and love her again (3:1), and he did. This shows how God loves us and how a man of God should love others.

Hosea found Gomer on an auction block, being sold as a slave to other men. They would use her anyway they chose, because she was a harlot. He bought her for himself and brought her home to love her again (3:2-3) and to give her another chance to be his faithful wife.

Hosea shows what true love is all about. Even though his wife had abandoned him and his children and was going to bed with every man she could, he still loved her. When he found her being sold to other men, filthy with the scum of sin and with the marks of the hands of other men all over her body, he still loved, forgave her, and accepted her back into his home. He cleaned her up and restored her to the family.

That is what being a Christian is all about – love, forgiveness, and acceptance. Jesus didn't come to give His life for us because we deserved it. God loves us so much that Jesus gave His life for us while we were still sinners (Romans 5:8).

We also should lay our lives down for others and learn to love each other in spite of our differences. We need to quit judging others by what they look like, what they have, or what they do or don't do.

We should accept others just as they are and forgive them for any and all offenses. If we judge, we will be judged (Matthew 7:1-2), and if we fail to forgive, we also won't be forgiven (Matthew 18:21-3 5).

God has instructed us to love in deed and in truth and not just in words (1 John 3:18). If we are asked to go one mile by someone, then we should go two (Matthew 5:41). If we see a brother in need and have the means to help him, we should help him. If we don't do it, then the love of God is not in us (1 John 3:17).

Beloved, let us love one another, for love is of God; and everyone who loves is born of God and knows God. He who does not love does not know God, for God is love (1 John 4:7-8).

And this commandment we have from Him: that he who loves God must love his brother also (1 John 4:21). By this we know that we love the children of God, when we love God and keep His commandments (1 John 5:2).

When people of the world hear of what is involved in loving the way God commands us to love, they sneer at it because they can't understand such a deep and sincere love. The reason is that they are of the world and not of God and, therefore, can't hear what God is saying (1 John 4:5-6).

We who are born of God should not have a problem with loving others the way God loves us and tells us to love others (1 John 4:7-8). If we do, then something is wrong.

When we were born from our mother's womb, we didn't know how to hate or how to be selfish. The easiest person to be loved and accepted by is a little child. They don't know evil yet. The reason is that our attitudes are taught to us as we grow up by the type of TV shows we watch, the people we hang around, and the things we are taught to do by everyone from our parents to our school friends and teachers.

Even a retarded child has much love in them because they are not filled with the selfish things of the world and can love with an unconditional love. This is why we must become as a little child again and be humble, to enter the kingdom of Heaven (Matthew 18:3-4).

A child is innocent and pure in mind and faith. If they are told something will happen a certain way if they do a certain thing, they will believe it and do what they are told, because they don't know how not to believe until they are taught.

When it comes to trusting God, if we would let go of all of our worldly ways of distrust and selfishness, we would all be happier and better off in every way. We would be relieved of all fear and doubt, because He will never let us down.

SOFT LOVE

It is much easier to give soft love than it is to give hard love, especially to someone who is close to us. Soft love is the kind of love we give when we want to help someone resolve their problems regardless of what God is trying to do in their lives at the time.

But we can cause more harm than good at times by giving people what they want or what they seem to need. If they are having problems in certain areas, such as paying bills, drinking, or drugs, they keep getting into trouble with the law, etc. and we keep bailing them out, then not only will they never come to maturity in that area, but we will be helping them stay the way they are.

When I go out on the streets, ministering to the homeless, and in the poverty-stricken areas, I meet hundreds of people who all have a sad story that would make the average person give them what money they can. But most of them are alcoholics and drug addicts. When they beg for money and people give it to them, all they do is buy another bottle of liquor or more drugs. The best way to help them is to give them a way to change their life.

We try to give them a place to sleep, something to eat, and a chance to be taught the right way of living, but many aren't interested. They have it made right where they are. They don't have to worry about paying bills or buying food because so many people are going out feeding them, thinking they are doing good, when they are really hurting these people. All they have to worry about is panhandling enough to get high again, so why consider changing, when all of their needs are being met?

This is a good example of when we should say no. Until they hit bottom hard enough, they won't want to change. When this happens, then we can give them soft love.

Another sad side to giving soft love, when we should be giving hard love, is that we lose our blessings from God. If we go out and do good deeds for others, and it wasn't God's will for us to do it, then we will have no rewards when we get to Heaven (1 Corinthians 3:10-15). God is not interested in how many good deeds we have done, or how well we can preach the Gospel; He is interested in how obedient we are to His commands. Obedience is better than sacrifice (1 Samuel 15:22).

When our short time on earth is over with, we will have to go through eternity with what treasures we have stored up while here on this earth. I try not to give or do anything else for anyone before asking God what His will is in their situation. If we aren't doing His will, then we are walking in rebellion to Him, and rebellion is as the sin of witchcraft (1 Samuel 15:23). Besides, He knows what the person needs to help him, and I don't, although sometimes I think I do.

HARD LOVE

Hard love is just as important as soft love and sometimes more important, if it is what they need. Hard love is when we say no, if yes would only hinder the person's growth.

Hard love is not only hard love because it is being tough with someone, but it is hard to say no to someone that we are really close to and care a lot about. It is easy to say yes, because we naturally want to do all that we can for those we love.

Even with our children, if they are misbehaving and we don't spank them, then we are doing them harm by not loving them enough (Proverbs 13:24). It is discipline through hard love that will get the foolishness out of them (Proverbs 22:15).

We must learn to do what God wants us to do more than what our flesh wants us to do. If we don't come to the place of loving God more than ourselves, we will not be able to say NO when we should, and we will end up in rebellion to God's commands.

Only through choosing to love God with all of our heart, soul, mind, and strength (Mark 12:30) will we be able to live right. Otherwise our own emotions will get involved in every situation, and we will have sympathy instead of empathy.

Also, if we don't love God with all of our heart, soul, mind, and strength, we will store up treasures on earth instead of Heaven, because we will put our worldly desires ahead of our heavenly desires and will, therefore, arrive in Heaven with nothing.

CHAPTER 10

The Life of a True Disciple of Christ

When I was of the world, I lived a life of total crime. I sold drugs, pimped women, robbed people and businesses, and did many other wrong things for a living. The cause that I was fighting for was worldly possessions that sooner or later would be lost in the same world it came from. I was willing to lay my life down for something that I thought was worth it, because it was something that I wanted.

The Life of a True Disciple of Christ

When I met Jesus, I knew that all of what I had lived for and believed in was worthless compared to Him and what He had to offer. When I asked Him to be my Lord, I took Him seriously and forsook all, so that I could be His disciple (Luke 14:33) and follow Him. I enlisted in His army and joined the other soldiers of Christ with a mission to take the world, with the promise that He would be with us wherever we went (Matthew 28:18-20).

To be a true disciple of Christ, the price is high and, as the Bible tells us, we must count the cost before we begin (Luke 14:26-35). A true disciple of Christ will be persecuted, ridiculed, slandered, jailed, beaten, and possibly even killed, spreading His Word. None of that matters to us because our love for God is stronger than any fear that this world could possibly bring on us.

Man can only harm our body, which will only turn back to dust in the end, but God can destroy both soul and body in Hell (Matthew 10:28). We choose to fear God rather than man.

As Christians, there are certain jobs that we have to turn down and/or quit because of sinful activities that are involved in them, such as lying, cheating people, selling pornography, the lottery, liquor, etc. We even lose jobs sometimes because it comes to a point of choosing to either continue in the straight and narrow path that is pleasing to our Lord or giving in to man's way of doing things.

A true disciple will lose fellowship with some friends and relatives because they refuse to do things that displease God, and their friends want to continue in sin. Outside of witnessing to them, we have to leave because we love Him too much to participate or even be around when those activities are going on.

Instead of being selfish and greedy, we do our best at all times to walk in the image of Christ, who died to meet the needs of others and served all as was needed. Because the love of God abides in us, if we see a brother in need and we are able to meet that need, then that is what we do (1 John 3:17-18). We do our best to love our neighbors, just as we love ourselves, because this is the will of our Father (Mark 12:31).

We have fallen head over heels in love with Jesus and, therefore, will do anything He tells us to (John 14:15). No sacrifice is too great for our Lord. He is worth every moment of our life. He died for us, therefore we will live for Him.

Many times we are made as uncomfortable as possible by Satan and man but we still choose to follow Jesus. We spend every waking moment searching to find what would please our Lord. We pray that every breath we take and every step we make will bring joy to His heart.

It breaks our heart, and we know it breaks the heart of Jesus, to look around and see so many people going to Hell and hurting, with no hope, nothing to eat, and no place to go, and the so-called Christians are sitting in a nice big comfortable home, with money in the bank, and are unwilling to take time out and use their possessions and show the love of Jesus to the world.

We, as Christ's followers, invite the homeless into our house and let them take a hot shower and feed them a hot meal. We then spend time explaining to them about this magnificent Jesus and how much He loves them.

The Life of a True Disciple of Christ

When it is time to go to bed, some of us even let them sleep in our beds, while we sleep on the sofa or the floor. We don't want to just tell them how wonderful He is. We want to do as Jesus says to do and love them as we love ourselves (Mark 12:31).

We choose to lay our lives down for them (John 15:13), just as Jesus did for us. Oh, how we wish we could spend all of our time telling people about Jesus and winning souls for Him. How we long to do nothing but build up His Kingdom and work with all of our heart for Him. We love Him so much. He is so worthy of all we have to give.

We seek His Kingdom and righteousness first (Matthew 6:33) and live by faith in God. We trust in Him to meet our every need, as we pray to Him. We have made a career of winning souls and making disciples for God over a worldly career.

Sometimes we scrape to make ends meet, and at times our ends only meet because of His faithfulness to meet all of our needs according to His riches in glory, as He promised He would (Philippians 4:19). Many times we must pray our needs in, as they come up, but He always hears and answers our prayers.

There are, however, many times when He blesses us in one way or another, and we have over and beyond our needs. Either way, we take what we have and use it to the best of our ability, to further His Kingdom, in an effort to love and serve Him. When we stand before Him, we want to hear Him say, "WELL DONE, GOOD AND FAITHFUL SERVANT."

We take every penny we make and do our best to use it the way He wants us to. We have chosen to make Him Lord of ALL in our lives, including our time and money.

Many times we don't have the time or money to go to eat in nice restaurants, buy the best in clothing, homes, or cars (unless He tells us to and provides the money to do it with). Every penny we have and every minute we are on earth is His, and we want to be a good steward of it. If we live in this way, He will give us much in Heaven (Luke 12:42-44).

He also makes it well worth it all to us in this life. In return for our devotion to Him and faith in Him, He gives back a hundredfold of what we give Him (Mark 10:30). He blesses us with very nice clothes and cars, we eat in very nice restaurants, and He meets all of our needs.

We are true fanatics for Christ. We are, as some say, fools. But we have found that the kind of fool we are now, which is a fool for Christ, is much better than being the fool we used to be (1 Corinthians 3:18-19), which was a fool for the world or Satan (which is the same thing), and being a fool for Christ has much bigger rewards.

There is only one love and one desire that totally rules and controls our lives, and that is the love that we have for our Lord. We desire to do all that we can to carry out the mission that He gave His life for, which is to save as many people as possible from going to Hell.

We live to worship and praise Him, to let Him know how much we love and appreciate Him. We serve Him with all of our heart, to tell Him that He didn't do it all for nothing. Even though none go with us, still we will follow Him.

Our belief of what life should be about is not accepted by the world, or by many Christians. We have found the way to total peace and security, by giving all which is involved in our lives to serve God.

We have become as a little child (Matthew 18:3-4). We have no cares or problems outside of doing the will of our heavenly Father and trusting in Him to meet all of our needs.

If we are sick, He heals us. If we need money or anything else, we tell Him and trust in Him to meet our need, wait on Him to direct us, and obey Him with no questions, when He tells us what to do. He always comes through for us.

Because we have chosen this life with our Lord, we have a lot of trials and tribulations, but we are totally happy serving Him, and we wouldn't trade it for all of the money in the world. We now feel fulfilled. We have a worthy cause and purpose in life.

When times get hard, and discouragement sets in, when it seems at times that we can't go on, we cry out to God. The Holy Spirit, who is our best Friend on earth, is always right there to comfort us and strengthen us, so that we can go on.

When we get beat up by Satan, the world, or man, God faithfully reminds us that what we are doing is needed to help the lost and hurting to find the way while time remains, and that we are pleasing Him by obeying His commands. He refreshes us by loving us, until we get our strength back, so that we can go out again, serving Him with all of our heart.

God has given us power over all evil (Luke 10:19). He has given us power to heal the sick and cast demons out of people (Mark 16:17-18). When we speak in the name of the Lord Jesus, He honors us, because we do and say all things according to His will to the best of our ability (John 12:26).

The Holy Spirit is so loving and powerful. He is always there to talk to us and show us the right way to go. We love Him and appreciate Him so much.

Even when everyone else turns against us and says or does things that hurt us, we know that we can always count on the Holy Spirit to be there with us. He is our best Friend. He will never leave us, nor forsake us (Hebrews 13:5) because He loves us just the way we are, even when we make mistakes. It is through Him that we are able to do all that we do. He is the Spirit of God, and we can do all things through Christ who strengthens us (Philippians 4:13).

We have chosen to make Jesus Lord of our lives. He is the reason we live, breathe, walk, talk, sleep, and eat. He is our happiness, excitement, and every-thing else that is good in life.

We work during the day for Him and dream of Him at night. He is the first one we think of and speak to when we wake up in the morning and the last one before we go to sleep at night.

He gives us joy that is so great to speak of (1 Peter 1:8) and fills our hearts with every desire pleasing to Him (Psalm 37:4). We truly love Him with all of our heart, soul, mind, and strength (Mark 12:30), and it is worth everything to serve Him.

The bond between us never weak-ens, but it grows stronger every day, because the more we get to know Him, the more we fall in love with Him. We have come to realize that we don't have to fight and struggle to hold on to Him in fear of losing Him. It is not we that have Him, but He that has us.

The Life of a True Disciple of Christ

We know that He loves us so much that He will never let us go. Nothing can ever separate us from Him except us choosing to let go of Him and go the other way.

We love Him so much that we find it hard, if not impossible, to carry on a conversation without relating it to Him. We know that He is the answer to all of our problems, and we want others to know it too. He has told us to go and tell all, so that is what we do.

We cannot have any meaningful relationship with anyone, whether friend or family, who doesn't love and/or believe in Him. He is the force which both drives and guides our lives.

We try to evaluate everything we see, hear, and feel, according to the Word of God and by what we understand to be His perfect will concerning the subject, because we know that His ways are perfect.

Handcuffed to Jesus

We do our best to handle each and every situation the way He would want us to handle them. Although we are not perfect, as He is perfect, and we make a lot of mistakes, it is comforting to know that through His grace we are covered.

Therefore, although we still fall short of the glory of God, by saying or doing the wrong thing at the wrong time, His grace is sufficient and enables us to go on to learn and grow to be more like Him.

Many of us come close to getting beaten and some of us do get beaten, attempts are made to stone us (and some do get stoned), and we are verbally abused by both non-Christian and Christians alike. We are asked to leave and not return to certain types of churches, because of the love and devotional worship we give to our God.

Curse words are spoken over us because we chose to continue following

The Life of a True Disciple of Christ

God the best way we know He wants us to and not the way others think we should. We continue to follow Jesus, doing all that He tells us to do, the best way we can.

We are willing to go to jail and even give our lives if necessary for our Lord. Our only prayer is that we will know what His perfect will is at all times, and we put our trust in Him to keep us in it. We know beyond a shadow of a doubt that all of His promises are true.

I remember the first time I ever went on a fast to seek direction from the Lord. It was my first supernatural encounter with His power. I went into the woods to camp out and fast for four days. I would pray all day and sing and dance around the campfire at night, worshiping Him. On the third night, as I was singing and worshiping Him, it began to rain. I looked up and saw that the sky was pitch black, and it was getting ready to pour. I cried out to God in confusion and said, "Lord, what is this? I came out here to seek You, and now it's going to rain?"

Then the Holy Spirit spoke out to me and said, "You will do the same works Jesus did and greater (John 14:12), and He calmed the storms" (Matthew 8:26). So I stood and lifted my hands toward the sky, and in the name of Jesus, I commanded the clouds to hold the rain. Then I took a step further and went for doing a greater thing by commanding the sky to clear. It reminded me of the dividing of the Red Sea. Within minutes, all of the clouds were totally cleared out of sight, and the sky was absolutely clear. I knew at that moment what God had given us as His children.

From there, I went out and spread the Gospel, healed the sick, led the lost to salvation, and set the captive free by casting out the demons that were in them.

When I was ministering in a park in New York City, a very skinny man with off-colored skin who had AIDS came up to me and told me he was dying. He could barely stand up and could hardly talk. I told him about Jesus, and he received Him as his Lord. Then I said to him, "I have some good news for you. You are a child of God now, and God can totally heal and restore you right where you are standing. Do you believe that?"

He said, "Yes."

I then told him I was going to lay my hands on him and pray for him, and the Holy Spirit was going to fall upon him and heal him, and he agreed. I prayed for him and broke all curses off of Him, cast out every demon the Holy Spirit revealed to me, prayed healing and restoration in the name of Jesus, and let him go and stood back and watched.

As I was watching him, his whole countenance changed, his skin color came back, his speech became clear, and it seemed as if God had put an air hose on him and blew him back up to normal size. He began moving around, with his whole being revived. He looked down at himself and then back at me with amazement, and said, "Hey, man, I feel good!"

I pointed my finger at him and said, "You're healed in the name of Jesus." This man who could hardly walk began running all around that park, telling everyone what God had done.

God told me to begin holding Bible studies in homes, and through prayer God would heal everything from toothaches to cancers. There were people who were supposed to get an operation for cancer, but when they got to the hospital the doctors couldn't find any trace of their malignancy.

I have come face to face with evil spirits that were so strong they made the hair on my body stand up, and chills would run up and down my spine. But when I told them they had to leave in the name of Jesus, they would turn tail and run.

Through the power of the Holy Spirit, in Jesus' name, I have cast demons out of people that threw them on the floor, and they went into convulsions. In the end, however, the demons had to leave.

We don't care where we have to go or what we have to do to set people free from Satan's hold. We'll do it with no fear of the demons, only faith in Jesus.

Many people say that we are over-zealous, but we refuse to compromise in any way from what we believe is our Lord's perfect will. We try, to the best of our ability, to serve and love Him with our whole heart, to be steadfast and immovable in His ways (1 Corinthians 15:58), to be ready, in season and out of season, to do His will (2 Timothy 4:2) and not to worry what man says, does, or thinks about us (Matthew 10:28). We are only concerned about what God thinks about us. We will continue to trust in Him to correct us, through those over us, the Holy Spirit, or some other source, when we are wrong, and to make what is wrong right. We know that He loves and accepts us just the way we are, so we will continue to do what we believe He wants us to do, the best way we know how, trusting in Him for guidance (Psalm 23:3).

After all, it is Him we will have to give an account to for what we have done and not done (2 Corinthians 5:10). We would rather be His sheep who pleased Him than a goat who displeased Him (Matthew 25:31-46) and wasn't allowed to enter into Heaven.

We are what is called "being black and white" in our walk for Christ, meaning that we believe and live according to what is written in the Bible, to the best of our ability. We add nothing to it and take nothing away from it, because there is a severe penalty for doing so (Revelation 22:18-19).

We only see, care, and live for one thing and are consumed with this one thing. Whether we live or die, are healthy or sick, poor or rich, hated or loved doesn't concern us at all. The one thing that does concern us is to please God.

We have a passionate burning desire in our hearts for Jesus, to complete His will for our life. We live for Him and to carry out His will, which is to further His Kingdom. The Word of the Lord is a lamp unto our feet (Psalm 119:105), and where He tells us to go and what He tells us to do, that and that alone we will do.

Jesus has made us a light that was meant to shine throughout the land, and that is what we intend to be. We are consumed by His fire and burn for one thing, to spread the glory of God and to please Him in every way. In doing so, we are totally content, because our purpose in life is fulfilled by doing what God has called us to do.

If we cannot consistently do the will of our Father, we become miserable and cry out in desperation to be able to return to His perfect will. It is there that we find peace and joy.

If, for some reason, we can do nothing but lie in bed, we will pray and seek the face of God. We will do, from that bed, what we are able to do, in spiritual warfare, to stand against the enemy, so that God's will can be done on earth as it is in Heaven, as we wait for God to raise us up again.

If we cannot be on the front lines in battle, then we desire to do as Moses, Aaron, and Hur did on the hill in Exodus 17:8-13. We will hold the arms of the Church leaders up, by praying against the enemy and for the Church to have victory over the enemy so that God's glory will continue to flow.

When God created man, He gave us control and authority over the earth and all things upon the earth. We were created in His image and were given honor and glory. We were positioned just slightly lower than the angels (Psalm 8:4-8).

Handcuffed to Jesus

We lost position that through rebellion and sin, but through the life and sacrifice of Jesus we can, in a sense, regain dominion (Luke 10:19-20) by going out and claiming the lost for God's Kingdom and for our inheritance. We, as Christians, are actually partners with God in the world's redemption. Where we fail as God's partner is when we don't appreciate the calling God has given us.

We, as His disciples, hold the highest office that man can hold, by being a missionary for God. I wouldn't trade it to be President of the United States, because it would only be a foolish demotion. To be a missionary for God is a higher honor than to be President, king, millionaire, or any other position that the world thinks highly of.

As disciples of Christ, we are called to spread His love throughout the land.

The Life of a True Disciple of Christ

We must come to the place in our walk with Jesus of realizing that we are not called to fight with any authorities, whether they are governmental, political, or even ecclesiastical. We are to be as wise as a serpents and as harmless as doves (Matthew 10:16) in everything we do, by trusting in God to work His perfect will out in everything.

We are out there because we love Jesus, and we love the lost. Through the guidance of the Holy Spirit, we do what God has told us to do, under any authority, as long as it doesn't go against God.

We will be loyal to that authority to the point of compromising our walk with our Lord. When we come to that crossroad, we will not obey the authority of man and will gladly face whatever consequences come as a result of the decision we have made.

We are in the world, but we are not of the world (John 17:14-16). We are only passing through, as a pilgrim and a stranger, on our way to a better place (Hebrews 11:3-14).

We remain as honest as possible in all situations. We will tell you the truth at all times. We let our yes be yes and our no be no, because anything more is from the evil one (Matthew 5:37).

We refuse to lie under any circumstances, for the Lord says that all liars will go to Hell (Revelation 21:8). We refuse to do anything that is against God's Word, even if we are hoping good will come out of it, because it will be sin (James 4:17), and sin will reproduce sin.

We do our best to win souls for Christ and then disciple them whenever possible, just as He has commanded us to do (Matthew 28:19-20). When we are not able to disciple them, we will lead them to a good Spirit-filled church that will be able to take care of them.

When I was under a pastor, I submitted to whatever he would say, as the Lord has indicated. But now that I am over pastors, I only submit completely to the Board of Ministry God has surrounded me with and walk in agreement with them.

Though I work as closely as possible with a local fellowship, I refuse to allow any source to control me regarding what and how to do what God tells me to do, other than God Himself, unless I am working under another ministry. The Lord is my Shepherd (Psalm 23:1), and He leads me, not man.

I do respect and submit to the authorities of the local body, by listening to and taking into consideration whatever they have to say, but whether or not I obey what they say will be determined by what I and those around me feel God wants us to do.

When Maria, my wife, and I made the decision to follow Jesus, we counted the cost of being His disciple, sold everything we had, and bought the Pearl that He was offering (Matthew 13:45-46). We have lost many friends and associates as we chose to go higher with the Lord, because not many are willing to pay that price. It doesn't cost anything to become a Christian, but it costs everything if you are to be a Christian who is sold out to God.

The further you go, the more sacrifice it will take, and the higher you go, the fewer people will be with you. This means that you will be separated from more people, as well as from worldly things. You will suffer for Christ's sake in many ways, but your reward will be greater than anything you could imagine.

The Life of a True Disciple of Christ

We know the world is watching us to see whether or not we will complete what we started. If we don't complete it, we will be made a fool. Though the price was high, we still chose to pay it, and now all those who knew us in the world and were watching respect us and know that there must be something to Jesus for us to pay that kind of a price and stick with it.

Jesus told us the price before we started. He said that whoever doesn't forsake all that he has cannot be His disciple (Luke 14:33). The cost was everything, everything that we had, and everything that we were.

We had to give up everything and die totally to self. We did it, knowing we would be scorned, mocked, and left standing by ourselves at times. We knew that we would be stripped of everything by God Himself, and sometimes we would be wanting something and have nothing.

That is the price of the Pearl He told us about. It seemed high-priced, until we saw the Pearl for ourselves. Then we knew that no price was too great. He is worth all that we had and much more. Now that we know Him personally, it doesn't matter to us if we live or die, only that we live or die for Him.

We have asked Jesus to be Lord of our lives, which means we are not our own anymore. We are bought and paid for by His blood (1 Corinthians 6:19-20). For Him we live, and for Him we'll die.

Jesus said that he who loses his life for His sake would find it (Matthew 10:39). Now we know what He meant. We have found life. We are happier than we have ever been before. We have joy unspeakable (1 Peter 1:8).

JESUS IS OUR LORD!

Other Books Available for a Contribution to Help Maria Walton Carry on Guy's Work

1. *Walking with Jesus* (a booklet for newborn Christians which explains what to do now that they have accepted Jesus as their Lord) $4 (plus $2 shipping and handling). (A great book for evangelism, available at bulk-rate prices)
2. *Bought and Paid For* (a study manual and a workbook, which teaches what happened when you accepted Jesus Christ as your Lord and what you need to do to walk in His full power) $18 (plus $5 for shipping and handling)
3. *Christian Evangelism* (to learn how to win souls and train others) $18 (plus $5 for shipping and handling)
4. *The Ministries of the Holy Spirit* (teaches about the Holy Spirit and how to receive the full power of His gifts) $18 (plus $5 for shipping and handling)
5. *Commentary on Revelation chapters 1-11* (188 pages explaining each scripture piece by piece in understandable terms) $25 (plus $5 shipping and handling).

6. *Overcoming Anxiety, Stress, and Depression through Jesus Christ* (a proven and accepted Christian program based upon medical facts and the Bible that you can do at home to overcome these problems. The program includes 15 recorded lessons and 15 recorded sermons on how to get lifted up and live for God, a study book, and a work book for each lesson, a relaxation recording, which teaches you how to relax and enter into the peace and joy of the Lord, so you can sleep at night and deal with daily pressures in peace, and a set of carry cards, which you carry with you wherever you go, and when an attack begins and you can't remember what to do to stop it, you are able to just pull your card out and read it, and it will remind you of what you are learning to do. Within a short period, you are able to carry on through your day. Program is available for an offering of only $270 ($18 per lesson) (plus $15 for shipping and handling), to help feed our orphans and continue helping the needy.

Guy Walton passed from this life in 2016, his wife Maria retired from public service, and True Life Ministries closed its doors. If you would like to order one of these books, produced and published by the ministry they founded, please contact us:

McDougal & Associates
198896 Greenwell Springs Road
Greenwell Springs, LA 70739

info@thepublishedword.com
www.thepublishedword.com

www.ingramcontent.com/pod-product-compliance
Lightning Source LLC
Chambersburg PA
CBHW061722020426
42331CB00006B/1042